Charlotte Peck
Dec., 1956

gift to
Krista Johnson

Aug, 1976

FANNY

A Musical Play by
S. N. BEHRMAN and JOSHUA LOGAN
(Based on the trilogy of MARCEL PAGNOL)
Music and Lyrics by HAROLD ROME

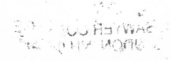

FANNY

RANDOM HOUSE, NEW YORK

Photographs by courtesy of Zinn Arthur

FANNY *was first presented by David Merrick and Joshua Logan at the Majestic Theatre, New York City, on November 4, 1954, with the following cast:*

(In order of appearance)

ARAB RUG SELLER	Mohammed el Bakkar
MARIUS, son of CESAR	William Tabbert
FANNY, daughter of HONORINE	Florence Henderson
MAORI VENDOR	Katherine Graves
LACE VENDOR	Betty Carr
CUSTOMERS	Toni Wheelis, Lindsay Kirkpatrick, Dolores Smith, Margaret Baxter
CLAUDINE } twin sisters, friends of FANNY { Tani Seitz	
CLAUDETTE } { Dran Seitz	
CHARLES	Wally Strauss
HIS FRIENDS	Bill Pope, Dean Crane, Ronald Cecill, Michael de Marco
NANETTE } { Norma Doggett	
MIMI } friends of FANNY { Carolyn Maye	
MARIE } { Ellen Matthews	
MICHELLETTE } { Jane House	
PANISSE, wealthy sailmaker	Walter Slezak
SAILOR	Herb Banke
THE ADMIRAL, an eccentric waterfront character	Gerald Price
MORROCAN DRUMMER	Charles Blackwell
SECOND MATE	Henry Michel
FISHERMAN	Steve Wiland
SAILMAKER	Jack Washburn
FISH-STALL WOMAN	Florence Dunlap
AN ARAB	Michael Scrittorale

CESAR, proprietor of café on waterfront Ezio Pinza
HONORINE, FANNY's mother, a fish-stall keeper Edna Preston
ESCARTIFIQUE, a ferryboat captain Alan Carney
M. BRUN, customs inspector recently
  returned from Paris Don McHenry
ARAB DANCING GIRL Nejla Ates
NUN Ruth Schumacher
CESARIO Lloyd Reese
BUTLER Mike Mason
MAID Pat Finch
GARAGE OWNER Tom Gleason
PRIEST Ray Dorian
ACOLYTES Gary Wright, Daniel Labeille

Directed by Joshua Logan

Scenery and lighting by Jo Mielziner

Costumes by Alvin Colt

Dances by Helen Tamiris

Musical direction and vocal arrangements by Lehman Engel

Orchestral arrangements by Philip J. Lang

Musical continuity by Trudi Rittman

vi

THE PLACE: The entire action takes place in and around the Old Port of Marseille over a period of years. THE TIME: Not so long ago.

MUSICAL NUMBERS

ACT ONE

Never Too Late for Love	Panisse and Ensemble
Cold-Cream Jar Song	Panisse
Octopus Song	The Admiral
Restless Heart	Marius and Male Ensemble
Why Be Afraid to Dance?	Cesar
Danced by Cesar, Marius, Fanny, Ensemble	
Never Too Late for Love (Reprise)	Cesar, Panisse and Honorine
Shika, Shika	Arab Dancing Girl, Rug Seller, Ensemble
Welcome Home	Cesar
I Like You	Marius, Cesar
I Have to Tell You	Fanny
Fanny	Marius
Montage	Fanny, Marius, Cesar, Ensemble
The Lovers	
The Sailing	
Oysters, Cockles and Mussels	Ensemble
Panisse and Son	Panisse
Wedding Dance	Danced by Charles Blackwell and Ensemble
First Act Finale	Ensemble

ACT TWO

Birthday Song	Fanny, Honorine, Ensemble
To My Wife	Panisse
The Thought of You	Marius and Fanny
Love Is a Very Light Thing	Cesar
Other Hands, Other Hearts	Fanny, Cesar, Marius
Fanny (Reprise)	Cesar, Fanny, Marius
Montage	Ensemble
Be Kind to Your Parents	Fanny, Cesario

Cesario's Party (Cirque Français)

Acrobats—Charles Blackwell, Michael de Marco, Ray Dorian, Bill Pope, Toni Wheelis
Pony and Trainer—Wally Strauss, Steve Wiland
Trained Seals—Dran and Tani Seitz
Living Statues—Betty Carr, Ronald Cecill, Norma Doggett, Ray Dorian, Ellen Matthews, Dolores Smith
Clowns—Herbe Banke, Mike Mason, Henry Michel, Jack Washburn
Finale—Aerialist, Dean Crane and Ensemble

Welcome Home (Reprise)	Cesar, Panisse

ACT ONE

ACT ONE

The Waterfront of Marseille.
The curtain rises. It is dawn on the waterfront.
The Bar de la Marine is at the left with an exterior ter-
race and small tables and chairs.
To the right, down stage, there is a kiosk. This is a fish stall
where HONORINE *and* FANNY *sell their fish.*
In the center is the sail shop of PANISSE, *a stucco-front*
building on which large metal letters are appliquéd: PANISSE.
At first we can see nothing through the fishnet curtain. Off
stage a voice calls.

VOICE

Marius! Marius!
> (*A shadowy, dimly lit figure leaps on the stage. In a*
> *moment we shall see that it is the* ADMIRAL, *a dark,*
> *lithe man in a tattered and strange version of an ad-*
> *miral's uniform. One old epaulette is pinned to his*
> *shoulder and he drags behind him a sort of duffelbag*
> *which is full of odds and ends of trash.*)

ADMIRAL

Marius! (*The* ADMIRAL *looks out front at something far*
away. He is very excited. He goes up and knocks at the bar)
Marius!

3

FANNY

MARIUS
(Off stage)
What is it, Admiral?

ADMIRAL
Get out of your bunk! I've got something to show you!

MARIUS
(Off stage)
Ssh . . . Don't wake Father!

ADMIRAL
His window's still dark! Hurry up! Hurry up!
*(He comes down stage, looks out front again and sings
excitedly to himself)*
>I'm in love with an octopus,
>A curly, girly octopus.
>I'll be true to her lips of blue
>And those eight loving arms around me!
>Those slippery cold,
(Boys enter)
>Wiggly bold,
>Eight loving arms around me!
(Some FISHERMEN have entered.)

FISHERMAN
Good morning, Admiral. *(The ADMIRAL salutes him. He returns the salute)* When are you going to get me a girl?

ADMIRAL
When you are rich.

FANNY

FISHERMAN

What about that beautiful Arab dancing girl?

ADMIRAL

I'm saving her for a captain.

SECOND FISHERMAN

Oh! What have you got for a poor fisherman?

ADMIRAL

Sympathy.

FISHERMAN

Marius isn't rich, but he's your friend—and I'll bet you would get him any girl he wanted.

ADMIRAL

Marius wants more than girls. (*Points to sea*) That's his mistress—the square rigger—the *Malaisie*—and I'm going to get *her* for Marius. (MARIUS, *a dark, vibrant, sensitive young man, enters. The* FISHERMAN *shrugs and goes to work on his nets. The* ADMIRAL *calls*) Marius!

MARIUS

What's up, Admiral?
    (*He sits on crate and puts his shoes on.*)

ADMIRAL

Look what just came into the harbor!

5

MARIUS

A square-rigger! I didn't know there were any left in the world. Look at the sun on those sails! Pink!

ADMIRAL

I've been talking to some of the crew. It's a scientific expedition going all around the world to study winds and tides. Think of it—five years under sail—the decks heaving under you! Tonkin . . . Macassar!

MARIUS

The isles beneath the winds! Ah!
(*At the thought of being on that ship and seeing all those far places he feels an acute visceral pain of longing.*)

ADMIRAL

(*Knows what he is feeling*)

Marius!

MARIUS

I want to be on that ship! Oh, God, I want to be on that ship!

ADMIRAL

I've invited some of the crew to come to Hakim's Cellar. Sailors will do anything for the Admiral if I get them girls. Don't go on torturing yourself. Let me get you a berth on that ship.

MARIUS

(*Looks up at the window of the bar*)

Shh!

6

ADMIRAL

Forget your father! My father didn't let me go to sea, and look at the result.

(FISHERMEN *laugh*.)

MARIUS

I'm all he's got, Admiral. I'm to inherit his bar. I'm to get married. I'm to settle down. I'm caught here. Ships will come and go and I'll still be serving drinks and wiping tables and listening to the gossip from the fish stalls.

ADMIRAL

It's not your father, Marius. It's little Fanny.

MARIUS

(*Rises*)

Yes, it's Fanny too. I stand behind that beaded curtain just to watch her smiling at her customers. I think about her at night. I say to myself, "In the morning, when Fanny opens the fish stall, I will go over to her and take her in my arms and tell her that I love her." And then when morning comes I see the harbor, I smell the tar they're putting on the hulls, (FISHERMEN *nod*) and God help me, I forget Fanny . . . Father . . . everything . . .

(*He sings*)

I see a silver bird that streaks the sky
And off we fly,
My heart and I,
My restless heart and I.

(*Sits on crate*)

I see a cloud dance by and fade from view
There we go too.
My heart and I,
My restless heart and I.
    (*Chorus*)
I say to each new ship that sails the bay,
"Are you the one it will be?
Have you come at last
This golden day
To set us free?
Take us away with you," we cry.
My restless heart.
My restless, restless, restless, restless, restless, restless heart
  and I.
    (*During the latter part of the song, the sun is coming
    up. There is a noise off stage of singing and dancing.*
    MOHAMMED, *an Arab Jack-of-all-trades, a* DANCING
    GIRL *and* SECOND MATE *enter.*)

ADMIRAL

My Arab girl! She's done it! She's got some of the crew
from the *Malaisie!*

DANCING GIRL

Admiral, this is the second mate of the *Malaisie.*

ADMIRAL

Second mate!
    (*They shake hands.*)

DANCING GIRL

He's coming to see me dance.

8

SECOND MATE

So you're the famous Admiral! Have you got any more cruisers like her in your fleet?

ADMIRAL

Come along and we'll open up Hakim's Cellar.

DANCING GIRL
(*Indicating* MARIUS)
Bring him too. He is nice.

ADMIRAL

Later—later! (*He shoves them off*) Marius, that was the second mate, the one who hires men for the crew. Come with us.

MARIUS

It's Father's day off. I'm on duty at the bar.

ADMIRAL

Can't you sneak away? This is a chance in a million!
(*Enter* HONORINE, *the ample, blowsy proprietress of the fish stall.*)

HONORINE

What's going on here? Nothing good, I'm sure.

ADMIRAL

Ah, Madame Honorine—the duchess of the fish stalls!

HONORINE

Riff raff!

9

ADMIRAL

(*Sings*)
I'm in love with an octopus
A slinky, inky, octopus
(*To* MARIUS)
I'll come back for you.
(*Continues song*)
Those wiggly bold, slippery cold
Eight loving arms around me.
Bah!
(*He exits.*)

HONORINE

That man's crazy and he's going to get you in trouble if you don't look out.

MARIUS

Where's Fanny?

HONORINE

Putting fish in the tank. Marius, your father's worried about you, and he's right. Let me tell you something . . .

MARIUS

Oh, excuse me, I forgot to start the coffee.
(*He runs out.* HONORINE *looks after him angrily.*)

CUSTOMER

(*At the fish stall*)
Are these the largest oysters you have?

FANNY

HONORINE

If you want sea monsters, go to the aquarium! (*Calling off stage*) Fanny! Bring some more oysters!
(FANNY, *a lovely young girl, enters.*)

CUSTOMER

These are better. I want two dozen.
(HONORINE *hands the woman two already-filled paper cones of oysters.* CUSTOMER *exits.* FANNY *is looking over at* CESAR's *bar.*)

HONORINE

(*Noticing* FANNY)
He's making some coffee! Fanny, stop dreaming about that boy! He doesn't even know you're alive!

FANNY

He does too! He must, Mama! It's just that he's shy.

HONORINE

He's shy! He's this! He's that! But he never speaks. He's tongue-tied! Fanny, you're eighteen years old and still not married. Why don't you marry young Victor? He's got pimples, but at least he has proposed.

FANNY

I don't like Victor, Mama—not that way.

11

FANNY

HONORINE

Well, I'm tired of selling oysters! I want to eat some for a change. If you don't get married, I'm going to have to do it myself.

FANNY

You?

HONORINE

Don't be surprised! I still get burning looks across my fish stall that almost bake the oysters! (*Holds up letter*) I got a letter from Panisse. He says he has something of an intimate nature to discuss with me—and he's rich and he's a widower. I'm going home to put on my new dress. That should turn the trick. (*Starting off stage*) Fanny, do you know what's the matter with our family? The wrong person is eighteen years old!

(*She exits dancing.* FANNY *is alone. Pause. Two young girls come in.*)

CLAUDINE

Fanny! Fanny! Charles proposed to me last night while we were waltzing.

CHARLES

Beware of the waltz.

FANNY

I'll soon be the only old maid left. You'll have to show me some respect.

12

CLAUDETTE

Old maid! What about—Marius?
(CLAUDINE *stops her, calling her attention to* MARIUS.
Everyone turns and looks at MARIUS.)

CLAUDINE

Hello, Marius.

MARIUS

Hello, Claudette—everybody.

CLAUDINE

(*Taking* CHARLES' *arm*)
We're going to get married.

MARIUS

Congratulations! I'd like to offer you all a drink, but
Father's upstairs and I don't know—Oh, wait a minute! Here
comes Monsieur Panisse, he's always good for a treat. (PA-
NISSE *enters. He is rotund, jolly and very shrewd*) M. Panisse!

PANISSE

What a festoon of girlish beauty!
(*He pinches one of the girls.*)

GIRL

Please! What would your wife say?

PANISSE

(*Indicates a small black bow on his arm*)
Let that sink in! The badge of my bereavement.

13

FANNY

GIRLS

Not Madame Panisse! Impossible!

PANISSE

Three months today!

GIRL

Oh, we're so sorry to hear it.

PANISSE

But it's still as vivid to me as if it were . . .

GIRL

Perhaps you'd rather not talk about it.

PANISSE

I enjoy talking about it. It was right over there in the room
that adjoins my sail shop. Félicitie had prepared a garlic
stew, strong as the wrath of God with all the garlic and the
fish heads—a masterpiece of a snack—and she relished every
single mouthful. The next morning—I woke up single.

(*He gestures toward the mourning band.*)

FANNY

Mama and I miss her, Panisse. She was one of our best customers.

PANISSE

Ah, yes—fine woman—great worker. And yet, with all her
efficiency there was a gaiety, a jocularity! I used to chase her
around the dining room table—give her little nips and some-

times, for variety, miniature pinches. (*The girls giggle*) Tiny ones, out of sheer high spirits. I'll never recover from this loss. There's only one thing left for me to do.

GIRLS

Oh, no! Your sail shop—you have so much to live for.

PANISSE

My mind is made up! (*The girls are horrified*) I'm going to get married again as soon as possible!

MARIUS

Get married? You?

PANISSE

Did you think I'd remain single? Never! Bad for the circulation.

MARIUS

But at your age, do you still circulate?

PANISSE

My dear boy, love is not a question of age—it's a question of aptitude.
    (*He sings*)
        Never too late, too late for love.
        Though years go flying,
        One keeps on trying,
        Autumn gets dressed up to wait for love.
        Never too late for love.
        Its tender hunger

FANNY

Makes the night younger
Till you jump for the moon up above.
Long winter nights are great for love.
Never too late for ooh-la-la-la, ooh-la-la-la,
Never too late for love.

CHORUS

Fa la la la

PANISSE

Any time at all

CHORUS

Fa la la la, Tra, la, la, la

PANISSE

Love may come to call,

CHORUS

Fa la, fa la la la

PANISSE

Knock at your heart and say,
"Hey, let me in again.
Knock, knock,
Knock, knock,
Let's begin again!" with
Ooh-la-la-la!
Ooh-la-la-la!
Never too late, too late for love.

While years are turning,
Hearts keep on burning.
Wise men will slyly tempt fate for love.
Never too late for love.
Its tender passion
Always in fashion,
Seems to light up the night up above.
Over thin ice we skate for love.
Never too late for ooh-la-la-la, ooh-la-la-la,
Never too late for love!

Marius, wine for the young people! I'm feeling expansive! (*Everyone exits into the bar, laughing and calling their thanks to* PANISSE. *He stays behind and speaks to* FANNY *when they are alone*) Dear little Fanny, what a charming picture you make!
   (*He sings*)
      The sun is the god of the day,
   (MARIUS *enters and listens*)
      But turn from him your cool young face away,
      Lest in his hot passion he seeks
      To ravish the lovely rose petals that glow
      On your delicate cheeks,
      Your dainty, delicate cheeks!
   (MARIUS *applauds in a disparaging way and goes back into the bar.*)

FANNY

Marius! (*To* PANISSE) What a pretty poem, Panisse. Did you write it yourself?

FANNY

I copied it from the label on a cold-cream jar. But the great merit of poetry is not the poem nor even the poet. It's the knack of fitting it into the conversation—a bridge to a delicate subject. Did your mother get my letter?

FANNY

Oh, yes. She's been in a flutter all morning. You said you had something of an intimate nature to discuss with Mama.

PANISSE

And do you suspect what it is?

FANNY

Well, as Mama is a widow and you are a widower . . .

PANISSE

(*Indicating his mourning bow*)
Three months today!

FANNY

. . . I can only conclude that you wish to ask my darling mama to marry you.

PANISSE

A charming thought and quite accurate except for one slight modification. I wish to marry you!

FANNY

Me! (*She laughs*) You're not serious!

18

FANNY

PANISSE

(*Laughs*)

I am. Your mother is an admirable and abundant woman but she does not make the poetry on a cold-cream jar come alive for me. Do I have your permission to speak to her? (*He kneels before her.*)

FANNY

(*She is horrified and urges him to get up. He tries, but cannot rise until she helps him*)

You don't need my permission. You're old friends.

PANISSE

Then you authorize it?

FANNY

But Panisse . . .

PANISSE

(*Takes her hand*)

Ah, Fanny, if you only knew how my heart flutters when I stand beside you.

FANNY

I'd heard you had been to see a doctor.

PANISSE

This isn't a medical flutter—it's a personal flutter. Such a delicate little hand. What an agreeable sample of what the rest of you must be like. (*He keeps holding her hand.* MARIUS *enters and listens*) And the little necklace—is it gold?

19

FANNY

Oh, yes, it was my aunt's.

PANISSE

It looks gold from here. Oh, it gets golder and golder, and there's a medallion on the end.
(*He is now peeking down between her breasts.*)

MARIUS

What are you up to, you old billygoat?

FANNY

(*Frightened but pleased*)
Marius! Oh, Marius!

MARIUS

You seventy-year-old lecher!

PANISSE

I'm a young fifty-four and I'm on the verge of being insulted.

MARIUS

Leap the verge.

PANISSE

Fanny, hold my hat!
(*Hands it to her.*)

FANNY

Panisse!
(PANISSE *and* MARIUS *are nose to nose.*)

20

MARIUS

Lecher

PANISSE

Puppy!

MARIUS

Eunuch!

PANISSE

Ah, now you're changing your attack! (*Takes his hat from* FANNY) First I'm a lecher, then a eunuch. I refuse to argue with a man who is inconsistent. Fanny, let me know when your mother comes.
(*He exits.*)

FANNY
(*Shyly*)
What made you do that, Marius? You almost acted as if you were jealous.

MARIUS

Oh, it had nothing to do with jealousy. I didn't like the way he was pawing you. And if he knows what's good for him he won't try it again!
(*There is silence for a moment, then* MARIUS *looks off at the sea.* FANNY *sings*)
Does he know?
Does he know?
How long, how long I've loved him?
Is he thinking of me now?
Does he know?

Does he wake up with my name on his lips?
Does the mention of me make his eyes shine?
Am I his every thought
His very life
As he is mine?
(*This is interrupted by* CESAR, *calling from inside the bar.*)

CESAR

(*Off stage*)
Marius! Marius! Marius!

MARIUS

It's Father!
(CESAR *enters from bar. He is the Napoleon of the neighborhood—tremendously exuberant, humorous, confident.*)

CESAR

There's a man in the bar delivering forty-five cases of vermouth!

MARIUS

Didn't you tell me to order forty-five, Father?

CESAR

I said five! Four or five! Not forty-five!

MARIUS

(*Running into the bar*)
I'll take care of it, Father.

CESAR

Children are the poison of a parent's existence!

FANNY

Oh, Cesar, you don't mean that.

CESAR

Yes, I do! Marius is driving me crazy. He forgets everything, spills everything, he's always dreaming. And he disappears from the bar for hours at a time. Where does he go?

FANNY

I don't know, Cesar. (*Pause*) But he sees that crazy Admiral a lot. Maybe it's one of the girls the Admiral gets for sailors.

CESAR

A mistress? No, I think it's more than a mistress. His departures are too irregular. No woman would stand for it. The illicit affair demands regularity. Still . . . Fanny, don't let one of those bad girls get my boy.

FANNY

What can I do?

CESAR

You love him, don't you?

FANNY

Sh—!

CESAR

He's got to find out some way. Go after him! Do you know how long I've wanted you to marry my boy? Since you were no taller than a pot of flowers!

FANNY

I've tried to show him how I feel, but . . .

CESAR

You are too subtle. Men are very stupid. First you've got to show them that you love them, and then you've got to explain to them that they love you.

FANNY

Maybe I'm just not a very exciting kind of person. Maybe I'm just sort of wholesome—and no man wants a wholesome girl.

CESAR

They do after they are married.

FANNY

Perhaps you're right, Cesar. I'm going to change my tactics and be a bold, brazen hussy!

CESAR

That's right—just like your mother! I'm sorry!

FANNY

Cesar, I hesitate to suggest this, but perhaps the trouble with Marius is you. You're a very strong person, Cesar. Perhaps you overwhelm him.

CESAR

Me overwhelm Marius? I am the most reasonable, patient, even-tempered man in Marseille—which means in the whole universe!

MARIUS

(*Coming from bar*)

You see, Fanny, Father believes Marseille is the center of the universe!

CESAR

It is the center—the center! I am here. That's north, that's south, that's east and that's west. Here—center!

MARIUS

But there are other places, Father.

CESAR

Yes, but they are off center! Marius, is it conceivable that a boy could want more than you have got right here?

MARIUS

Yes, Father, it's conceivable.

(*Young people come on stage.*)

25

GIRL

Marius, why didn't you come to the dance last night?

CESAR

Where did you go?

MARIUS

I went walking on the sand bar.

CESAR

Sand bar!

GIRL

Maybe he's afraid some girl will dance away with him.

CLAUDINE

I think you're right. Marius is too shy to dance.

CESAR

(*Takes* FANNY *in his arms*)

What are you afraid of, Marius? You're perfectly safe on a dance floor. Isn't he, Fanny? (*Rushes to* MARIUS) Most innocent pleasure there is. You're out in public and you're fully dressed. (*Music*) What could happen?

> Why be afraid to dance, to dance?
> It's just polite and nothing more.
> Why be afraid to dance, to dance?
> Hold someone tight around the floor.
> Just a social convention
> All nice people recognize.
> No flirtatious intention,

DANCERS

Merely lovely exercise!

CESAR

So why be afraid to step and whirl,
To dip and twirl,
To hold a girl?
Nothing to do with romance!
No! So, why be afraid to dance?
(*At the finish of the dance,* CESAR *looks at his watch
and runs out.*)

MARIUS

Right on the dot.

GIRL

What do you mean?

MARIUS

This is father's day off, and this is the time he starts getting dressed up to visit his lady love.
(*The young people disperse.*)

HONORINE
(*Off stage*)

Fanny!

FANNY

It's Mama!

27

HONORINE

(*Enters*)

How do you like my dress? (*Enter* PANISSE *from sail shop*)
Panisse, give me your honest opinion.

PANISSE

You look like a great lady visiting the poor!

HONORINE

Fanny!
 (*She signals* FANNY *to go.*)

MARIUS

Oh, dear!
 (*Runs off stage.*)

PANISSE

Well, Honorine, did you get my letter?

HONORINE

(*Sits on crate*)

Yes, and I read between the lines.

PANISSE

You see, Honorine, I'm sure that in spite of my age . . .

HONORINE

Don't let age worry you. You're a bit old for me, but I
can make the adjustment.

28

FANNY

PANISSE

Maybe I'd better write you another letter.

HONORINE

Are you proposing marriage to me or not?

PANISSE

I am proposing marriage, but not to you.

HONORINE

Not my little . . .

PANISSE

Exactly. Your agreeable daughter, Fanny.

HONORINE

But she's not out to be adopted!

PANISSE

I'll give your daughter a dowry of a hundred thousand francs. She'll have everything—money, servants, jewels . . .

HONORINE

But won't she still be missing something?

PANISSE

When she's married to a man who has six hundred thousand francs?

HONORINE

But nightgowns have no pockets, my good man!

PANISSE

Don't underestimate Panisse!
(*Enter* ESCARTIFIQUE, *spherical, complacent and obtuse.*)

ESCARTIFIQUE

Panisse!

PANISSE

Escartifique!

ESCARTIFIQUE

Look who just came back from Paris. He was on my ferry
boat.
(*Enter* BRUN, *tall, thin and scholarly.*)

PANISSE

Ah, Brun!
(ADMIRAL *enters.* MARIUS *goes to him.*)

HONORINE
(*Rises*)

Welcome home!

ESCARTIFIQUE

Now we can have our card games again!

BRUN

Who has Cesar been cheating while I've been away?

PANISSE

Mostly me.

MARIUS

(*To* ADMIRAL)
I'll be right with you. M. Brun! Welcome home!

BRUN

Marius! Where's your father?

MARIUS

Father? This is father's day off. He's coming downstairs on
his way to visit his lady love.

BRUN

Does he still pretend to be going anywhere but where he's
going?

PANISSE

All the same old elaborate explanations, but he doesn't
fool anybody. Come, let's have some fun with him. Sit down,
everybody.
(*They all sit.*)

BRUN

Is it still the voluptuous Dutch lady?

MARIUS

There's a new one. She's Spanish—and monumental!

BRUN

Here comes Cesar.

CESAR

(*Enters from bar*)
Well, think I'll stretch my legs a bit.

MARIUS

Good idea, Father.

CESAR

No particular place in mind. Might have a stroll along by the aquarium . . . visit the Museum of Natural History . . . or take in the monuments.

ESCARTIFIQUE

I'd like to take in those monuments myself.

PANISSE

You want us to know, Cesar, that if something comes up we can find you either at the aquarium or at the Museum of Natural History—or will you be between the two?

CESAR

I might. Or I might decide to have a bowl of fish soup at the Caruso Bar—take a table for one on the terrace and watch the people go by.

ESCARTIFIQUE

All the various nationalities—Moroccan, Greek . . .

FANNY

Spanish!

ESCARTIFIQUE

Si, si, Señor!

CESAR

The air is crackling with innuendo. Am I on trial? What kind of an inquisition is this?

PANISSE

Spanish!

CESAR

Well, if it makes you feel any better, your double-edged remarks have completely spoiled my whole afternoon! Now I don't even know where to go—and I am late.
(*He starts off stage.*)

PANISSE

Never too late, too late for love.
(CESAR *stops, turns and glares at them, then starts again.*)

HONORINE

Though years are turning,
Hearts keep on burning.
(CESAR *stops again, turns and glares, then starts once more.*)

33

FANNY

Over thin ice we skate for love.
Never too late—

CESAR

(*Stops, thinks a moment, then smiles and sings*)
For ooh-la-la-la, ooh-la-la-la,

PANISSE and CESAR

Never too late for love.
Never too late, too late for love.
Though years go flying,
One keeps on trying.
Autumn gets dressed up to wait for love.
Never too late for love!
Its tender hunger
Makes the night younger
Till you jump for the moon up above.
Long winter nights are great for love
Never too late for ooh-la-la-la, ooh-la-la-la!
Never too late for love!

(CESAR *and* PANISSE *go off in opposite directions as the curtain goes up on the next scene.*)

Scene II

Hakim's Cellar.

In the darkness we see a nearly naked girl dancing. When the lights come up we see that it is Hakim's Cellar, a dark, cavern-like café where the sailors in Marseille go. Sailors and girls surround the beautiful belly dancer.

The ADMIRAL *enters and a* SAILOR *calls to him.*

SAILOR

Hey, Admiral! Here's our second mate!

ADMIRAL

(*Goes to the* SECOND MATE, *shakes hands with him, turns and calls off stage*)

Hey, Marius!

(MARIUS *enters, wearing a little straw boater. He crosses to the* ADMIRAL.)

DANCING GIRL

(*As he passes the dance stand*)

Your name Marius?

ADMIRAL

(*To* SECOND MATE)

This is my friend Marius—feel the muscles in his arm! (*The* SECOND MATE *feels* MARIUS' *arm while* MARIUS *watches the dance*) Will you give him a berth on the *Malaisie?*

35

SECOND MATE

I'd rather give her one.

ADMIRAL

Maybe I can arrange that for you, Mate!
(*The* DANCING GIRL *finishes her dance. A* SAILOR *tries to kiss her, but the* ADMIRAL *takes her from him and passes her to the* SECOND MATE. *The* SAILOR *attacks the* SECOND MATE. MARIUS *defends the* SECOND MATE, *and is in turn attacked by another* SAILOR. *A general melee develops and moves off stage.* FANNY *has entered and watched the fight. The* ADMIRAL *notices her.*)

ADMIRAL

Fanny! You followed us here!

FANNY

What are you doing to Marius?

ADMIRAL

Saving him from you.

FANNY

Is that Arab girl his mistress? Is that why he's here?

ADMIRAL

Put Marius out of your mind. Marry Panisse!

FANNY

I will never marry Panisse!

ADMIRAL

This is no place for a girl like you. Get out of here!

FANNY

I'm not afraid of you! Something terrible is happening to Marius and I'm going to stop it!

ADMIRAL

Get out! Get out!

FANNY

I'm going to stop it! I'm going to stop it!
    (*She runs out.*)

SECOND MATE

(*Entering, followed by* MARIUS)
That boy of yours is a great fighter!

ADMIRAL

Didn't I tell you he was strong?

SECOND MATE

I can use him on the *Malaisie!* (*Hands papers to* MARIUS)
Here's your berth! We sail at dawn for five years!

ADMIRAL

Calcutta!

MARIUS

Tonkin!

ADMIRAL and MARIUS

Ahoy!

(They go. The music and dancing resume. Through the curtain, the lights come up on the next scene and the dancers disappear.)

Scene III

Cesar's Bar.
Night. MARIUS *enters, followed by the* ADMIRAL.

MARIUS

It's all right, Admiral. Come on in. I'm sure Father's asleep.
I'd never live through tonight if I had to face him.

ADMIRAL

I'll come by early in the morning to get you on board.

MARIUS

All right. I'll start packing my duffelbag now.
(*The* ADMIRAL *starts to go.* CESAR's *voice is heard outside.*)

CESAR

Good night, Panisse. Thanks for the champagne.

MARIUS

Don't let him see you. Climb out of my bedroom window—and while you're in there hide these papers under my pillow, will you?
(*The* ADMIRAL *goes into* MARIUS' *bedroom.* CESAR *enters from the street.*)

CESAR

(*Hangs up coat and cane*)
Good evening, Marius.

FANNY

MARIUS

Good evening, Father. Did you enjoy yourself at the museum?

CESAR

Museums are very exhausting places.
(He is looking around the room.)

MARIUS

What are you looking at?

CESAR

The furniture. Some day, Marius, you will be old enough to know that the best thing about going away is coming back. (MARIUS *smiles and sits*) You don't believe me, do you? That's because you're very young.

CESAR

Why, even when I leave this neighborhood for only a
    day,
To go to the beach or the vineyards across the bay,
No matter what I do or see,
After turning home again,
I get to that corner and then,
Sweet voices,
I hear sweet voices calling to me!
Welcome home, says the street,
As I hurry on my way.
Welcome home, sings the gate, like a song.
Welcome home, says the door,
Glad to feel your hand once more.

Now you're back where you belong.
Welcome home, says the chair,
Holding out its friendly arms.
Welcome home, says the bed, rest on me.
Now you're back where you should be,
Close your eyes, close your eyes,
And the world will settle down to size.
Welcome home, says the lamp,
Lighting up familiar things.
Look around at your friends good and true.
Get your cares all untied,
While you're warming up inside,
Welcome home to you.
Welcome home to you.

This isn't a place to go away from. It's a place to come back to—a quiet place where things are manageable—where there's a routine you can roll up in like a blanket (*slaps* MARIUS' *cheek*) and the air all around you is humming a familiar song.

Welcome home, ticks the clock,
Now it's time to get undressed.
Welcome home, says the floor to your shoe.
Then you turn out the light
And the darkness says good night.
Welcome home to you . . . my son,
Welcome home to you!

(*Putting shoe on*)
Marius, Panisse just told me you and he had a fight about Fanny today. So that's your secret, hm? Fanny! Well, I ap-

prove! I've been hoping for years that this would happen. And don't worry about a place to live. Do you think I'm going to live alone like some stupid old animal? No! You and Fanny can have my big room upstairs. I'll take your little bedroom down here and some day, who knows . . .

(*Cradles an imaginary baby*)
La la la, la la la
La la la la la la la—

MARIUS

Father, it's not true about Fanny and me.

CESAR

Not true. (MARIUS *shakes his head*) Then why did you act like a madman when you saw Fanny with Panisse?

MARIUS

I don't know. Something came over me. But what you think, it's not true.

(*To avoid his father's eyes, he begins cleaning the bar.*)

CESAR

Well, that's the first time I ever pried into your personal affairs, and I promise you it's the last. Give me the petty cash, and before you go to bed, tighten the tap on the big wine cask. It gets loose.

MARIUS

(*Pouring petty cash into bag*)
I'll take care of it.

CESAR

Reassure me on one point, Marius.

MARIUS

What?

CESAR

It's not one of the Admiral's girls, is it?

MARIUS

Father, I may not have told you the whole truth, but I have never lied to you. It's not any girl. It's . . . (*Music: "To the Sea"*) . . . it's nothing I can talk about now. (*Replaces cash drawer.* CESAR *starts off stage*) Father . . .

CESAR

Yes, son?
    (*Music: "I Like You."*)

MARIUS

Thanks for being so concerned about me.

CESAR

Good night, son. See you in the morning.

MARIUS

In the morning! Father . . .
    (MARIUS *sings*)
        I like you,
        Like you very much,

43

More than I could ever show.
I like you.
It's not much to say,
But I need to tell you so.
Sometimes you wait to say things,
You wait too late.
Days that once seemed so slow,
How fast they go!
Words spoken
Never mean too much,
Still I just want you to know
I like you.

CESAR

Marius, it's not your fault. I've been impatient with you, but now I'm going to talk to you man to man. (*Seats him in chair*) I'm going to make one more effort to beat into your head how to make a vermouth cassis.

(*Goes to bar, puts cassis bottles on table.*)

MARIUS

Now?

CESAR

Now! (*He seats* MARIUS *in a chair and starts to mix a drink*) One third vermouth—and twist the bottle to trap the last drop. Now, man to man, one small third cassis—and trap! (*Above table*) Two large thirds bubbles . . . (*He sings*) La la la la la la . . .

(*He fills glass with seltzer.*)

44

MARIUS

That makes four thirds.

CESAR

It depends on the— (*He calms himself*) It depends on the size of the thirds! (*He finishes mixing the drink, hands it to* MARIUS *to taste, then pushes* MARIUS *to the bar and motions him to mix a drink.* MARIUS *does so, but very clumsily. As he pours the seltzer he imitates* CESAR *singing La la la la la la. When he splashes the seltzer all over the table,* CESAR *stops him*) You will never learn to make a vermouth cassis—but nevertheless, this has been a very important step in our lives. We have finally talked to each other. You know . . .
  (*His hands are on* MARIUS' *shoulders*)
  Sometimes you wait to say things,

MARIUS and CESAR

  You wait too late.
  Days that once seemed so slow,
  How fast they go . . .

CESAR

You have often heard me say that children are the poison of a parent's existence, but that cannot be entirely true because, my son, no matter what you decide to do or why you do it—
  I like you!
  (CESAR *gives* MARIUS *an embarrassed shove and goes quickly into his room.* MARIUS *stands a moment, overcome, and then replaces the cassis makings on bar*

*and starts to close up the bar for the night. He turns
out the lights. Suddenly* FANNY *appears in the door.
She comes into the bar.* MARIUS *closes the shutters behind her and then goes to her. She is very upset.*)

MARIUS

Fanny! Fanny, what is it?

FANNY

I have to, I have to, I have to tell you
I have to but I don't know where to start.
I have to, I have to, I have to say
What I'm shouting in my heart.
(*Embraces him*)
I love you, I love you,
I'll always love you.
Love you, want you, need you
My life through!
I've said it, I've told you, and now forget it
Unless you have to say it too.
Maybe you do.

MARIUS

Oh, Fanny, I'm so divided—so torn!

FANNY

Is that Arab girl your mistress? She's very exciting. But
maybe I could learn to be exciting too—if you'd help me.

46

MARIUS

Come here, Fanny. Sit down. (*Seats her*) Wait a minute.
(*He goes into his room, returns with a box from which he
takes a sea shell. He kneels before her*) The Admiral and I
went walking on the sand bar when I was twelve years old.
We met an old man with a beard like a snowstorm. He said,
"Looking for sea shells, son? Here's one you'll never find
anywhere. It was the house of a sea animal that disappeared
from the earth five thousand years ago." Then he told me
about the isles beneath the winds where black trees grow,
and when you cut them they are gold inside—and smell of
camphor and pepper. That's when it happened—this deep,
painful wish I have. It makes me dizzy, as though I were
falling forward always . . . toward the sea. I have despised
myself for not going before, and now I know why. It's been
you.

(*He sings*)
Only you, long as I may live, Fanny, Fanny, Fanny,
You, long as I may live, Fanny.
If I could love, that's what I would say.
But my heart isn't mine to give, Fanny, Fanny, Fanny.
No, no, not mine to give, Fanny,
For it is gone, given long away.
To the sea, my one love
In her gray green clothes,
Deep with wonders beyond the shore.
To the isles 'neath the winds
Where the spice wood grows.
I must know them all or sleep no more!
(*Turns to her*)

47

Here's a boy with no heart to give, Fanny, Fanny, Fanny.
Not worth one tear you'll cry, Fanny!
Oh, Fanny, good-bye!
    (*Music continues.*)

FANNY

Good-bye! You're sailing on the *Malaisie!*

MARIUS

Tomorrow morning!

FANNY

Five years!

MARIUS

Please don't try to stop me, Fanny!

FANNY

Marius, if you want to go to sea, I want it for you. If that will make you happy, I send you! It's all so dreadfully clear now . . .

I love a boy with no heart to give!

MARIUS	FANNY
Fanny,	No heart
Fanny, Fanny!	To give!

FANNY

Worth every tear I'll cry!

MARIUS

Fanny! Oh, Fanny—

48

FANNY

Fanny . . . Fanny . . . Fanny! I'm not going! I can't leave you!

(They kiss passionately. Then he leaves her and walks up to the bar. She follows him and embraces him. They kiss again, then look up as they hear CESAR *in his room.* FANNY *leads* MARIUS *into his bedroom. As* MARIUS *closes the door behind him,* CESAR *enters and watches them leave. He makes a step forward, excitedly, then takes* MARIUS' *vermouth cassis from the bar and lifts it in toast toward the bedroom door. He sings)*

CESAR

Fanny! Oh, Fanny!

(He drinks the vermouth cassis. As he lifts the glass, the lights fade and the curtains close.)

Scene IV

The Dock.

A group of SAILORS, WIVES *and* CHILDREN *enter. The* SAILORS *are leaving, and* WIVES *and* SWEETHEARTS *are kissing them good-bye and waving. The singing chorus sings an arrangement of "Fanny."*

The ADMIRAL *enters, dragging* MARIUS *along with him.* FANNY *enters.* MARIUS *turns and looks sadly at her, then turns and exits with the* ADMIRAL.

The curtains part and we see the Malaisie in full sail through the morning mist. It sails across the stage and slowly disappears as all the people on stage sing "Restless Heart" and wave to the departing ship.

CESAR *enters, holding* MARIUS' *straw boater, shouting "Marius . . . Marius" as the boat disappears.*

The curtains close and we see only the solitary figure of CESAR, *still clutching* MARIUS' *hat, while the chorus at one side sings:*

> Sometimes you wait to say things,
> You wait too late.
> Days that once seemed so slow
> How fast they go . . .
>
> *(The chorus disappears as the lights of the next scene come up slowly through the curtain on the next scene.)*

SCENE V

Cesar's Bar.
Daytime. PANISSE, BRUN *and* ESCARTIFIQUE *are in the bar.*
CESAR *is standing down stage, and as the curtain opens revealing the bar, the three men speak to him.*

BRUN

Come on, Cesar, let's finish the game!

PANISSE

Yes, we've waited long enough!

BRUN

Either throw Marius' hat away or stick your fist through it. You should have done it two months ago when he flew the coop. Escartifique, it's your play.

ESCARTIFIQUE

This is an important play. It requires thought.

PANISSE

Then you'll lose.

ESCARTIFIQUE

Now let me see—should I lead a spade or a heart?

CESAR

(Clutching at his heart)

Ooh!

ESCARTIFIQUE

What's the matter?

CESAR

I had a slight clutching at my *heart,* like you do when you eat too much—a flutter of the *heart.*

ESCARTIFIQUE

A flutter of the . . . Would you like some wine?

CESAR

No, you idiot, I would not like some wine! Wine is not good for the *heart!*

ESCARTIFIQUE

I just thought . . .

CESAR

Wine is bad for the *heart!*

BRUN

(Slams down his cards and rises angrily)
In a championship match you'd be disqualified for that!

CESAR

(Innocently)

For what?

PANISSE

You are not even allowed to say "hello" to a friend.

CESAR

I know, but if a friend should come in, I would hardly have the *heart* not to . . .

PANISSE
(Rising)

They are cheating!

ESCARTIFIQUE
(Rising)

Do you accuse me of . . .

CESAR

Not you, stupid! You haven't got the brains!
(ESCARTIFIQUE *sits.*)

BRUN

Panisse, you watch Escartifique. I'll cover Cesar.
(BRUN *and* PANISSE *sit and watch the other two closely.*)

CESAR

This is humiliating. It reflects on my integrity.

PANISSE

That's right. I suppose it hurts your feelings.

CESAR

Hurts my feelings? It practically breaks my *heart*. Isn't that true, Escartifique? He breaks our *hearts?*

ESCARTIFIQUE

(*Finally gets* CESAR's *idea*)
Breaks our . . . Yes, yes, I am stupid! (*He replaces card he was about to play and selects another instead*) There!

PANISSE

(*Puts down his cards again*)
This game does not count.

CESAR

Why?

PANISSE

Look into your own *heart* and you'll see why! By God, you must take me for a fool!

ESCARTIFIQUE

I thought it was very clever the way he did it.

PANISSE

I don't play cards with you any more. You are a cheat and a hypocrite!

CESAR

(*Rises and goes over to him*)
If you are not careful, you are going to insult me.

FANNY

PANISSE

Good! That's been my ambition ever since we were school-
boys and you bullied me all over the waterfront!

CESAR

Bullied you? I put up with you!

PANISSE

Put up with me! I was your little slave! In school when
you had to stay in during lunch and write two hundred times,
"I was naughty," you made me write it while you ate my
lunch.

CESAR

(*To* BRUN *and* ESCARTIFIQUE *as he pokes* PANISSE *in the
stomach*)
I ask you both, did he need any lunch?

PANISSE

I made a list of all my grievances and I swore that when I
grew up I would beat him to a pulp—and do you know what
this bully did about that? Grew up first! (*To* CESAR, *furiously*)
Good-bye!
(*He storms out.*)

CESAR

Good-bye!
(*Walks over to where* MARIUS' *straw boater hangs on
the wall.*)

55

ESCARTIFIQUE

We must have patience with old Panisse—chasing after a young girl for ten weeks and nothing to show for it but complete exhaustion.

BRUN

(*Rises*)
Cesar, stop mooning at that hat.

CESAR

If you think I am upset because my son abandoned me, you are crazy! I have forgotten him!

BRUN

And I suppose if he wrote you a letter you wouldn't read it?

CESAR

I certainly would not.

POSTMAN

(*Entering*)
Good afternoon, Cesar. Letter and a newspaper for you.

CESAR

Give the newspaper to me. Drop that over there anywhere.
(*The* POSTMAN *gives* CESAR *the newspaper and puts the letter on the bar.* FANNY *enters.*)

FANNY

Anything for Fanny Cabanis?

POSTMAN

No, nothing. (FANNY *is stricken*) Don't blame me. I carry the letters—I don't write them.

(*He goes out.* FANNY *starts to follow him.*)

BRUN

There's one for Cesar.

FANNY

Where? (BRUN *points to the letter on the bar. She picks it up*) Calcutta! From Marius! (*She goes to* CESAR *who is reading his newspaper*) Aren't you going to read it?

CESAR

Read a letter when I've got all this exciting news in *The Bartender's Journal?*

(*Goes back to his paper.*)

FANNY

Cesar, open the letter. Please.

BRUN

Yes, open it!

ESCARTIFIQUE

Stop bluffing!

CESAR

Cluck, cluck, cluck! I'm going in the kitchen where I can read in peace.

(*He goes into his room.*)

FANNY

(*Pushing* BRUN *and* ESCARTIFIQUE *out*)
He'll never read it while we're all here.

ESCARTIFIQUE

Couldn't we steam it open?

BRUN

Come on! By tonight he'll be giving public readings of it at every street corner.

(*They go.* FANNY *goes back to the bar for the letter, but meanwhile* CESAR *has sneaked out and taken it into the kitchen.* FANNY *looks for the letter.*)

CESAR

(*Off stage*)
Fanny! (*He enters, rushing to* FANNY *with the letter*) Fanny! I happened to open Marius' letter by mistake, and Fanny, he's fine! He's happy!

FANNY

Happy?

CESAR

Yes! Well, I couldn't read it very well. Something seems to have happened to my eyes all of a sudden. Run over it again for me, will you? Sit down here.

FANNY

(Starts to read)

"My dear Father. Please forgive me for the pain I have caused you. I want you to know that I think of you every evening."

CESAR

Hmph! Thinks of me every evening. But I am stupid enough to think of him all day long too. Go on.

FANNY

"At first they made me assistant cook."

CESAR

(Laughs)

Assistant cook!

FANNY

"But after several days they replaced me."

CESAR

Naturally! They were all starving to death!

FANNY

"At Port Said, a sailor got some mysterious illness. They thought it was the plague . . ."

CESAR

The plague! I kept Marius at home for a month to avoid the measles, and now he's on a boat with the plague—the

59

Black Death! The neck swells up, the eyes pop out, the tongue hangs out like a beef tongue . . .

FANNY

"But they found out it wasn't the plague."

CESAR

Why didn't he say that sooner?

FANNY

"One of the scientists on board says that this passion I have to sail the seas is natural . . ."

CESAR

Hmm?

FANNY

". . . because I am from Marseille and therefore I must be descended from the Phoenicians."

CESAR

Nobody in our family by that name . . .

FANNY

"We are now engaged in measuring the depths of the Indian Ocean."

CESAR

What? Oh! This boy who could not even measure a vermouth cassis, now is measuring an ocean! (*Shaking his fingers in amazement*) Ai ai ai ai ai!

60

FANNY

"Please don't worry about me, Father. I'm as happy as a fish in water. I embrace you with all my heart. Your son, Marius."

CESAR

Your son, Marius . . .

FANNY

There's a postscript. "Please write me about Fanny—how she is and about her mar—"
(*She stops quickly.*)

CESAR

Why did you stop? (*He takes the letter and goes over to the window to read*) "—about her marriage to Panisse." Why does he say that? Fanny, I knew you were together that night and I felt so safe. Why did he go?

FANNY

The boat whistles of the *Malaisie* waked us. I could tell what he was thinking—but for this girl, but for this one night, I could be on that ship. Suddenly I felt that he would end by hating me.

CESAR

Why should he hate you?

FANNY

Because I tricked him—with the oldest trick in the world.

61

CESAR

Yes, it is the oldest trick in the world, Fanny. That's why it's so good.

FANNY

Do you know why I told him I was going to marry Panisse?

CESAR

Why?

FANNY

Vanity. Lying there beside him I felt I was irresistible to him. I thought I would test him.

CESAR

Women pick strange times to make men pass examinations.

FANNY

Well, there's one consolation, isn't there? He's as happy as a fish in water.

(*She breaks down crying.* CESAR *takes her in his arms as the curtains close.*)

Honorine's Kiosk.

HONORINE *is busy selling her shellfish to the townsfolk in front of her shellfish stand. The stage fills with people who are colorfully dressed and having a lively time.*

CHORUS

Oysters, cockles and mussels,
Fresh alive from the blue,
Bite them quick or they might start biting you!

A FISHWIFE

Honorine?

HONORINE

Yes, dear?

FISHWIFE

Do you think it's going to be lively today?

HONORINE

I certainly hope so.

A CUSTOMER

These oysters aren't firm!

FANNY

HONORINE

Stop massaging them. They've given in! (*Chorus sings another phrase of "Oysters, Cockles and Mussels."* FANNY *appears looking very upset*) Fanny, did you see the doctor? (FANNY *nods*) Was I right? Do you need a tonic? (FANNY *does not answer*) Fanny, what is it?

FANNY

(*Throwing her arms around* HONORINE)

Mama!

HONORINE

You're going to have a child! Oh, my God in heaven, it's not true!

FANNY

Oh, Mama, it's true!

HONORINE

You dishonest girl! It's lucky your father's not alive—this would kill him!

FANNY

Beat me! Do anything, but let me stay with you!

HONORINE

Don't come to my home or you'll find the door locked! Go! Walk the streets! (FANNY *sways*) Oh, my God, you're going to faint! (*And she does faint*) Don't die, my baby! I forgive you anything! Just don't die! (FANNY *comes to a bit*) Who

64

was it? Marius? (FANNY *nods*) Oh, that Marius, with his dreamy eyes! Now we know what he was dreaming about! (*A sudden thought*) Oh, my God! The oysters I forced down his throat! When can we expect this disgrace?

FANNY

In March.

HONORINE

Perfect! The month of march hares and lunatics. Thank the good Lord my mother is tucked away in her grave. Well, she always did sleep through every crisis.

FANNY

Mama! Mama! What am I to do?

HONORINE

Do? Marry Panisse! He asks for you every day.

FANNY

Couldn't I go on earning my living and not marry anyone —raise my baby with the money I can put aside?

HONORINE

We would have to move away. The disgrace . . . The disgrace . . .

FANNY

But Panisse won't marry me when he finds out.

HONORINE

He mustn't find out! Don't bother Panisse with details like that!

FANNY

But if I don't, it would be cheating him. Now you're asking me to be a cheat.

HONORINE

Now you're giving *me* lessons in virtue! Besides, you can't be sure you're having a baby.

FANNY

The doctor told me.

HONORINE

Doctors make mistakes. It's probably something in the air —some little virus. Besides, why tell the truth when it might not even be the truth?

FANNY

If it's not the truth then I don't have to get married.

HONORINE

You can get married without being pregnant. Lots of girls do it. (*She rises.* FANNY *embraces her*) No, I'm not going to kiss you until you're married!

FANNY

I'll go to Panisse! I'll go now!

FANNY

HONORINE

Your sacred word you won't tell him!

FANNY

My sacred word!
> (HONORINE *gives her a shove and she runs off stage.*)

A FISHWIFE

Lots of activity, Honorine! Wonderful day!

HONORINE

Lots of activity! Wonderful day!
> (*She staggers off stage, weeping, as the lights come up on the next scene.*)

Panisse's Sail Shop.
PANISSE *is behind the counter, checking over his books. A*
WORKMAN *is arranging some sailcloth on the floor.*

PANISSE

What are you looking at, François?

WORKMAN

Little Fanny Cabanis is standing outside.

PANISSE

Fanny? Take this order to the loft. And don't disturb me.
(*The* WORKMAN *goes off.* PANISSE *goes to the door*) Come in
out of the sun, little Fanny. (FANNY *enters. He seats her*) I
hear Cesar had a letter from Marius.

FANNY

Yes. Marius is very happy. He's not coming back.

PANISSE

Fanny, you haven't come to say that . . .

FANNY

Yes, Panisse, except . . .

68

FANNY

PANISSE

Except that you hesitate because of you and Marius.

FANNY

What do you mean?

PANISSE

Fanny, the morning Marius sailed I was up early in front of my shop. I saw you climbing out of his bedroom window.

FANNY

Oh!

(*She covers her face.*)

PANISSE

Don't feel bad about it. Fanny, when a man of my age marries a young girl, the scales are not quite in balance. She is bringing him her youth and beauty, all fresh and new, and what is he bringing? A home, comfort, affection . . . but also a gray mustache—well, tinged with gray. Is that a harmonious composition? But if the young girl has been discreetly indiscreet, the equilibrium is somewhat re-established.

FANNY

Oh, Panisse, how nice you are! I would work like a slave to make you happy. I would be a servant to you.

PANISSE

Servant? You will be my wife if you will accept me.

FANNY

I accept you, Panisse.

PANISSE

Oh, my cup runneth over! Fanny, I'll devote myself to you so completely—I'll be so tender, so considerate—I'll make you so happy that you'll forget all about Marius. In fact, when he returns you'll invite him to dinner and he'll be like a stranger to you.

FANNY

(*Suddenly overcome*)
No, Panisse! I can't invite him to dinner!

PANISSE

What is it, Fanny?

FANNY

I can't marry you, Panisse! And I'm very sorry I ever said I could.

PANISSE

Why not?

FANNY

I haven't even the right to kill myself!

PANISSE

You're going to have a baby!

70

FANNY

Don't tell Mama that you know and that's why you re-
fused me.

PANISSE

Does anybody else know about this?

FANNY

The doctor.

PANISSE

Doctors can't talk because they're doctors, and mothers
can't talk because they're mothers! Anyone else?

FANNY

No one, I swear.

PANISSE

Fanny, could you promise me that the whole world will
think it's my baby?

FANNY

Do you mean you still want me—now?

PANISSE

Oh, Fanny, now more than ever! Oh, Fanny, our baby will
have everything! We'll give him everything!

FANNY

And if it's a girl?

FANNY

We'll give her almost everything! Besides, that's very unlikely. There are only boys in our family. Oh, think of all those old Panisses—aunts, uncles, cousins—with all their vineyards that stretch all over those hills all through the South of France. And there hasn't been a baby in the Panisse family for fifty years. They've all been counting on me!

> (*He sings*)
> It's very hard to have a child,
> My wife and I were driven wild.
> We asked advice from every side
> And what they told us to we tried.
> How we tried!
> Oh, oh, oh, oh, the diets we'd take,
> Candles we'd light,
> Trips that we'd make.
> Oh, oh, oh, oh, the hoping and then
> Starting the hoping all over again.
> We tried out all the health resorts,
> Went in for special winter sports,
> We ran to every shrine to pray,
> Did exercise the Swedish way,
> And other things I won't recall
> But nothing happened, not at all,
> Not at all, not at all, not at all!
> To have a baby's very hard to do,
> But now, I'll have a son, I'll have an heir,
> Thanks to you!
> *Panisse and Son*

72

Will look so fine!
Panisse and Son
Upon my sign!
Panisse and Son!
Oh, how those words will shine!
No better poetry
Could ever, ever be!
No words could mean as much to me
As those three!
You must have noticed my sign on the wall,
The letters over my store,
How they seemed crowded, all pushed to one side,
As if making room for more.
Now I've got something to show just to you,
A secret no one could know.
   (*He goes behind the counter and takes some big, brass*
   letters out of a drawer)
Look, Here's an "S"!
This is the "AND"!
This is the "N"!
This is the "O"!
And Son! And Son! And S-O-N!
Panisse and Son,
Displayed on high!
Panisse and Son,
For all to eye!
Panisse and Son
As they go strolling by!
Panisse and Son!
And Son!

FANNY

I can't believe it. My child will have a name!

PANISSE

In school when the teacher calls the roll and comes to the name Panisse, a boy will raise his hand and say, "I'm Panisse."

FANNY

I'm Panisse!

PANISSE

When is it due?

FANNY

In March.

PANISSE

March! The month of geniuses! (*Then figuring*) A seven-months' baby . . .

FANNY
(*Dismayed*)

Oh!

PANISSE

Rather makes me out to be a rake. (*A new thought*) What about Cesar? He must never know.

FANNY

Never! He'll be angry enough about the marriage.

PANISSE

Angry! He will explode into small pieces. Ha! Oh, how he looked down his nose at me when Marius was born and I couldn't have a child. Now we will pay him back for the years he has bullied me! Now King Cesar's rule is over! Poor old Panisse is chanticleer now! (*As he crows with delight,* CESAR *enters*) Welcome, Cesar!

CESAR

Honorine has made an absurd hint about a marriage.

FANNY

Panisse and I are going to be married.

PANISSE

And if you dress properly we may ask you to the wedding.

CESAR
(*To* FANNY)

It's your mother. Your mother loves Panisse's money and she has sold you like a little African slave!

FANNY

It's not Mama's decision. It's mine!

CESAR

Well, it's my decision that this marriage will not take place!

75

FANNY

PANISSE
(*Stepping to* CESAR)
And who is going to stop me?

CESAR
I, my dromedary, will stop it by destroying the bridegroom before he gets to the church.

PANISSE
Don't you bully me or I will tell you something that will shut your mouth forever! Your bullying days are over. This is my shop! My name is Panisse and she's going to be Madame Panisse! And what's more you extinct rooster . . .

FANNY
Panisse, be careful what you're saying!

PANISSE
And what's more, we're going to have a baby!

FANNY
Panisse!

PANISSE
And what's more, it's going to be a seven-months' baby!

CESAR
What!

76

FANNY

Panisse, please!

PANISSE

And do you know whose baby we're going to have?

FANNY

Be quiet!

PANISSE

We're going to have Marius' baby, that's whose baby we're going to have!
(*He snaps his fingers in* CESAR's *face and goes behind the counter.*)

CESAR

You're a mad dog and you ought to be shot.

PANISSE

Here's the gun. Shoot!
(*Takes gun out of drawer.*)

FANNY

Put the gun down!

PANISSE

But before you pull the trigger, know this—when you shoot me, you're shooting the father of your grandchild. You're shooting the husband of your poor grandchild's mother! Now, shoot!

77

FANNY

(He slams the gun down on the counter. It goes off, and across the room the sails on a model ship collapse.)

CESAR

(To FANNY)

Fanny, is this man gaga or is this true?

FANNY

(Turning away)

It's true.

CESAR

Well, then, everything's all right. Even if I have to send a telegram of six pages that will cost me a million francs, I'll send it—and Marius will come home at once. Oh, he'll be so happy to be a father. Oh, that Marius—he can't make a vermouth cassis, but— *(Shaking his fingers)* —ai ai ai!

FANNY

(Goes to him)

Oh, Cesar, you don't really think he'd come?

CESAR

Of course. Why not?

FANNY

He says he's as happy as a fish in water?

CESAR

Oh, that boy's so crazy, measuring the depths of that Indian Ocean.

FANNY

Cesar, I'm afraid. What if he won't come back?

CESAR

He will.

FANNY

What if he doesn't?

CESAR

I am almost sure he will.

PANISSE

When people ask me how much I'm worth, I usually lie to them. I tell them half a million francs. Actually, I'm worth a million and a half. I only bring this up now because it seems to fit into the conversation.

CESAR

Well, it doesn't fit me! I don't care if you're worth a billion francs, I'm not selling you my grandson. Come on, Fanny. Let's go. Come on.

(*Takes her arm.*)

PANISSE

Cesar, can you guarantee that Marius will come back in

time? Can you guarantee the winds and tides? Be very careful what fate you decide for your grandson. The child of Fanny Cabanis will be an illegitimate child, a shame and a disgrace to her family. But the child of Madame Panisse (*Music: "Panisse and Son"*) will be born in a wonderful old bed covered with fine linen sheets. (FANNY *turns and looks at* PANISSE) His closets will be filled with underclothes and sweaters which will be knit by cousins and aunts and great-aunts. There will be great joy in thirty families simply because a little child has been born—and that child will be enthroned on top of a family tree like a cross on a church steeple. (FANNY *pulls away from* CESAR, *weeping*) Is that position too high for your grandson, Cesar?

CESAR

No position is too high for my grandson. But the son of Madame Panisse would not be my grandson. I couldn't even brag about him. I'd have to smuggle myself in here at night pretending to be a casual acquaintance.

PANISSE

Fanny, a child's godfather could come to see him any time he likes—take him strolling in the park, alone—sport him around on his shoulder?

CESAR

Would the godfather be able to choose the child's name?

PANISSE

If he has a knack for choosing names.

CESAR

How do you like the name Marius? (FANNY *looks at them both*) Master Marius Panisse!

PANISSE

(*Thinks a moment*)
It has a certain ring to it. Not much . . .

CESAR

Not so fast! I have something better. An important man ought to have three names! Let's say his name is Marius Panisse. Couldn't we put a third name in front—for instance, Cesar? Cesar Marius Panisse!

PANISSE

And for a nickname—we could call him Cesario!

CESAR

Wait a minute! About this million and a half—would my godson inherit all of it?

PANISSE

Naturally. He'd be our son.

CESAR

With my bar thrown in, it would come to almost two million. Fanny, when your son is twenty years old he could smoke cigars as long as your arm!

(As they seal the bargain with a handshake, FANNY *puts her head down on their clasped hands and the curtains close.)*

Scene VIII

The Wedding.

A wedding bouquet is tossed onto the stage. WEDDING GUESTS *run on and one girl catches the bouquet.*

HONORINE, BRUN, ESCARTIFIQUE *and a* FISHWIFE *are among the group—all dressed properly for the occasion.*

FISHWIFE

Lovely wedding, Honorine!

HONORINE

Yes, wasn't it!

FISHWIFE

Fanny looked radiant!

HONORINE

Yes, didn't she!

FISHWIFE

Who would have thought . . . Fanny and Panisse!

HONORINE

I was completely bowled over! But now I'm adjusted to it and I think they'll be very happy—all three of us!

> (*The curtain opens revealing a pink and white striped wedding tent. There is a lively wedding dance, at the end of which* CESAR *enters the tent, followed by*

PANISSE *and* FANNY. CESAR *and* PANISSE *are in formal attire.* FANNY *wears her wedding gown.* CESAR *holds up his hands for silence.*)

CESAR

And now, the bride must dance with the groom!
(PANISSE *and* FANNY *dance as the wedding guests sing.*)

CHORUS

Why be afraid to dance, to dance?
It's just polite.
Why be afraid . . . Why be afraid . . . Why be afraid . . .
(*Suddenly the voices and music become discordant. The lights are dimmer. The people sway dizzily— even the tent itself sways.* FANNY *holds her hand to her head, confused, bewildered.* MARIUS *appears through the crowd, as if in a dream. The* ADMIRAL *is with him.* MARIUS *takes* FANNY *in his arms and she kisses him passionately.*)

FANNY

Marius, I was just dreaming I had married Panisse!

MARIUS

That must have been a nightmare.
(*They laugh quietly together and she holds him close to her.*)

FANNY

And here I am, married to my love . . . my love . . . my love . . .

84

MARIUS

How could I ever have longed for the sea?

FANNY

(*A sudden frightened cry*)

The sea!

THE CROWD

(*In the same cry*)

The sea!

(*A discord.* FANNY *falls back, frightened. The* ADMIRAL *takes* MARIUS' *arm and starts to lead him away*)

MARIUS	ADMIRAL
Marry Panisse! Marry Panisse! Marry Panisse!	I'm in love with an octopus, A curly, girly octopus . . .

FANNY

(*Calling after* MARIUS)

I was lying, Marius. I will never marry Panisse! (*The lights change and the tent appears normal once more*) But I have married Panisse! (*Turning to* CESAR) We are married, aren't we?

CESAR

Yes, you are married.

PANISSE

Waltz with me—it will start our new life together.
   (*He sings*)
        Why be afraid to dance, to dance?
        It's just polite and nothing more.

85

FANNY

THE CROWD

And nothing more!

FANNY

Nothing to do with romance!

EVERYONE

No! So, why be afraid to dance?
(FANNY *dances with* PANISSE. *Everyone joins in the dance, and as it reaches a climax the curtains close.*)

Scene IX

The Waterfront of Marseille.

The sound of Easter bells is heard. Two NUNS *cross and exit. The* DANCING GIRL *enters and crosses, accompanied by the* ARAB *and two* SOLDIERS. *They are drinking, laughing, as though after a night of celebration. A* PRIEST *crosses, followed by two acolytes.*

PRIEST

It's Easter! Hurry! We'll be late for Mass! Put that sling-shot in your pocket and pick up that incense.

(*The* PRIEST *and acolytes exit.*)

(*The curtain opens on* CESAR'S *bar and* PANISSE'S *shop. It is early morning.* PANISSE, *in an old-fashioned night-shirt and in bare feet, hurries out of his shop and across to the bar.*)

PANISSE

Cesar! Wake up!

(*A light goes on in* CESAR'S *window.*)

CESAR

(*Off stage*)

What is it, Panisse?

PANISSE

The little one is getting himself born!

CESAR

I'll be right down!

PANISSE

(Calling off stage)

Brun! Escartifique! The little one is getting himself born!
(BRUN *and* ESCARTIFIQUE *rush on.* CESAR *joins them,
still putting on his bathrobe. As they all go toward*
PANISSE's *shop,* HONORINE *rushes out. A crowd is beginning to form, all in night dress.)*

HONORINE

Fanny is well and the baby is here!

PANISSE

Is it a boy or a girl?

HONORINE

Good Lord, I forgot to look!
(*She dashes inside.* PANISSE *and* CESAR *rush in after
her. The crowd is still gathering, and by now the
stage is full. After a moment,* PANISSE *and* CESAR *run
out carrying a ladder and the brass letters of "& SON."
They put up the ladder against* PANISSE's *shop wall,*
BRUN *and* ESCARTIFIQUE *steadying it for them.* PANISSE
climbs the ladder and CESAR *passes him the letters
which he attaches to the wall next to the word "Panisse." As* PANISSE *attaches the last letter, the song
reaches a climax, and he comes down the ladder,
stands back to admire the sign, and throws himself
into* CESAR's *arms.*)

Curtain

ACT TWO

ACT TWO

SCENE I

The Nursery.

The scene is a baby's-eye view of a nursery.

FANNY, HONORINE, BRUN, ESCARTIFIQUE, RELATIONS, SERV-
ANTS *form a group and start singing directly to the audience.
We realize immediately that they are singing to the one-year-
old* CESARIO.

*This is a ten-part round. Finally, they are all singing at
the top of their voices, when* FANNY, *noticing that the baby
is asleep, gradually quiets them and sends them out.*

1. Panisse's son, hooray, hooray!
   Panisse's son, one year old today!
2. La-la-la-lu-la, happy birthday. La-la-la-lu, Cesario.
   La-la-la-lu-la, happy birthday. La-la-la-lu, Cesario.
3. Extraordinary child, best I've ever seen, really!
   Extraordinary child, looks to me like a genius.
4. Look at that hair, look at that stare, look at that mouth
   like roses.
   Look at that chin, look at that grin, look at how big his
   nose is.
5. Ooh! Ooh! Hear him talking. Ooh! Ooh! What's he saying?
   Ooh! Ooh! He said "Ma-Ma," I could hear him plain as
   day.

6. Looks just like his mother, anyone could tell.
   Not much like his father, which is just as well.
7. Coochy-coo! Coochy-coo! Very pleased to meet you.
   Coochy-coo; Coochy-coo! You're so sweet, I could eat
   you!
8. Hello, young man, my best felicitations.
9. You darling birthday boy, birthday boy. How are you?
   You darling birthday boy, birthday boy. How do.
10. He looks thin, much too thin, I tell you.
    He looks thin, much too thin. They should feed him
    more!

Scene II

Panisse's Living Room.
A comfortable, bourgeois room with a shuttered window
opening on the street.
Guests come through. CESAR *and* PANISSE *saying good-bye.*
HONORINE *takes the candle from the cake and puts both on a*
sideboard. SERVANTS *serve champagne.* FANNY *comes out of*
the child's room.

PANISSE

I tell you, Cesar, that boy is going to be a mechanical genius—fit president for our new motor company. Did you see
the way he handled that Mechano set?

CESAR

I certainly did. He tried to eat it!

PANISSE

He was testing the steel.

CESAR

He was tasting the paint. If you aren't careful, Fanny,
Panisse will poison him.

FANNY

If I'm not careful, Panisse is going to miss his train.

HONORINE

(Rising)

Panisse has appointments with the automobile people in Paris tomorrow. As bookkeeper for Panisse and Son I say don't miss that train!

PANISSE

Well, good-bye, everybody. I think you'll agree with me that my son's first birthday has been an historic occasion.

ESCARTIFIQUE

(Glass in hand)

I am just drunk enough to say, Panisse—and mind you, I wouldn't say it if I were sober—and before I say it I've got to thank you for the champagne that got me drunk enough to say it. You are a smug man.

PANISSE

Smug!

ESCARTIFIQUE

Well, smuggish.

PANISSE

Smug does not remotely convey what I am. I am arrogant. I am conceited. I'm Alexander the Great and Napoleon rolled into one. And why not? I've got Fanny. *(They all smile and nod)* And Fanny, I've had just as much champagne as Escartifique, in fact more. Because before the party I slipped

94

back into the nursery and had a bottle with Cesario. While
he was having his formula, I had mine.

    (*He sings*)
To my wife
Who walks so gently through my thoughts
All day long.
Clean and fresh and white,
Soft and strong.
Makes me feel
That there is nothing I can't do
If I try
With my wife and son
Standing by.
She may scold, say I eat too much,
Find some fault, give free advice.
But a meal needs that added touch of salt and spice.
To be extra nice.
Words won't do.
There's so much I must thank her for.
Where to start?
How am I to say
From the heart
What I owe?
To my critic, my partner,
The flavor of my life—
To my wife.
    (*Leans and kisses her*)

Fanny, a famous Greek philosopher once said a wife is one
who will stick by you through all the troubles you would
not have had if you hadn't married her, but I don't believe

that because every night and every morning when I wake up I raise an invisible glass—

> To the sunlight that brightens
> The autumn of my life,
> To my wife.
> (*The song ends and* PANISSE *goes off, putting on his hat and taking his briefcase. Everyone goes after him except* HONORINE. FANNY *returns.*)

FANNY

Go to bed, Mama. You must be tired. I'll finish the accounts.

HONORINE

Oh, no, you won't. Where's my bankbook? (*Picks up the account book.*) You look after your baby—I'll look after mine. Good night, dear.
> (*Pats the account book.*)

FANNY

Good night, Mama.
> (HONORINE *exits.* FANNY *is alone. She picks up some knitting. Street noises are heard outside. A drum. There is a noise at the window.*)

MARIUS

(*Opens the window. He wears a seaman's uniform. His face is bronzed.*)

Hello, Fanny!

FANNY

Oh, Marius!

MARIUS

Thought I'd drop by and say hello. I'm back for a few hours. Father was out. May I come in? (*He steps over the window sill*) The *Malaisie* is in Sydney in drydock. Three of us brought some precision equipment back for repairs. (*A pause. Takes hat off*) How are you, Fanny?

FANNY

I'm all right.

MARIUS

And Panisse? He must be very happy.

FANNY

Yes.

MARIUS

Then, it's all happened for the best. Very nice here. (*Drum stop.*) Big house. Dining room? (*Goes toward nursery*) What room is this?

FANNY

(*Quickly bars his entrance to the room*)
That's a little extra bedroom.

MARIUS

Oh, that's the baby's room. The Admiral told me you had a baby. Funny my father never wrote me about it. How old is your baby ?

97

FANNY

Oh, he's just a baby.

MARIUS

Why didn't you write me about him?

FANNY

You didn't write me.

MARIUS

I wrote five or six letters but I tore them all up.

FANNY

Why?

MARIUS

You were happily married to Panisse and—that didn't take long, did it? Two months after I sailed.

FANNY

Go now, Marius. Whatever you can say now can be of no use.

MARIUS

Why did you marry Panisse so quickly? Why didn't my father write to me that you had a son? And how is it that Panisse, who was never able to have a child with his first wife . . .

FANNY

Go away, Marius.

98

FANNY

MARIUS

How is it that this child was born less than seven months after your marriage?

FANNY

How do you know that?
(MARIUS *picks up the birthday cake and candle.*)

MARIUS

Because today was his first birthday! Oh, Fanny, I left you with a child. Forgive me.

FANNY

I forgave you long ago. Did you see the isles beneath the winds?

MARIUS

Yes.

FANNY

What were they like?

MARIUS

Have you ever seen photographs of the craters of the moon? That's what they were like—volcanic ash. Oh, Fanny, I left with such high hopes! Then . . .
(*He sings*)
The thought of you surrounded me, enfolded me.
I saw your face around me everywhere.
At night, instead of starlit waves, all I could see

Was you there—you there!
You—sweeping with your broom
You—standing at your stall.
You skipping down the dock
Smiling just to hear me call.
And then at once it happened very suddenly
As if some one had come and closed a door.
I searched and couldn't find you in my memory
No more—no more.

I'd forgotten what your face looked like. That's when I wrote
Father for your photograph—and it came—your wedding
photograph. Oh, Fanny, I couldn't look at you as a bride.
I only came back to see you again, hoping it wasn't too late.

FANNY

Don't, Marius! Don't say it!

MARIUS

(Sings)

I have to, I have to, I have to tell you,
I have to though I don't know where to start.
I have to, I have to, I have to say
What I'm shouting in my heart.
I love you, I love you,
I'll always love you.
Love you, need you, want you
My life through!
I've said it, I've told you, and now forget it,
Unless you have to say it
Unless you have to say it—
(They are in each other's arms. He is kissing her pas-

sionately when CESAR *bursts in and separates them. Loud music as* CESAR *enters.)*

CESAR

Now then, children, Panisse is a very decent fellow and he's not here. Don't make him look ridiculous in front of his family furniture. (*He looks at* MARIUS. *They are overcome. Music: "Welcome Home."* CESAR *embraces* MARIUS) Oh, you look good in that suit! Your old friend the Admiral told me you were here.

MARIUS

Father?

CESAR

Yes?

MARIUS

Why didn't you tell me about the child?

CESAR

(*Innocently*)
Child?—Somebody have a child?

FANNY

He knows, Cesar.

CESAR

Oh, that child!

MARIUS

(*Taking* CESAR's *shoulder*)
Father, it's very good to see you again, but right at this moment I beg you to leave us alone.

CESAR

No. During the absence of her husband you have nothing to do in the home of Madame Panisse. You're coming with me.

MARIUS

I'm staying here.

CESAR

Oh, no, you're not. There have been all kinds of people in our family—idiots, pirates, customs inspectors and even stubborn old bullies like your father. But there have never been any rats. Are you coming?

MARIUS

No.

CESAR

Then I am not going. We'll just have a nice conversation. What shall we talk about? (CESAR *sits and talks as they stand silently*) I see by the papers, the King of Montenegro arrived in Paris with twenty-six members of his household. Purpose of visit, to get his glasses fixed. And, incidentally, to see the girls dancing at the Folies Bergère. The king's problem is that until he gets his glasses fixed he cannot tell exactly

what sex the girls are. My heart goes out to his majesty. Well
now, let's see . . . (*The sound of a door slam*) The door!

FANNY

(Calling)

Panisse, you haven't missed your train again?

PANISSE

(Off stage)

I didn't miss it. I let it go. Ran into Doctor Cigalon and he
told me there's a whooping cough epidemic and I . . . (*He
runs in and sees* MARIUS) Marius!

CESAR

He's just here for a few hours.

MARIUS

That all depends, Father.

PANISSE

Depends on what?

MARIUS

It depends on you and it depends on Fanny.

PANISSE

Fanny is my wife and the mother of my son.

MARIUS

It's not your son, Panisse. Not really.

103

PANISSE

For a long time now I've been trying to go to Paris on business, haven't I, Cesar? (CESAR *nods*) I've missed every train. Every time I put my foot on the platform I would say, "This is the night Marius is coming back. What if he tries to take everything away from me." For two years I've been preparing my answer and now that I see you standing there so brown and tanned, I forget what I was going to say. Perhaps I'm in the way.

FANNY

No, Panisse!

PANISSE

Yes, perhaps I'm in the way and the most gracious thing for me to do would be to go out and drown myself by accident. And Fanny, believe me, if it would assure your happiness I might even do that. Only if I am dead I won't see the little one any more. So I absolutely refuse to drown myself.

CESAR

Nobody asked you to.

PANISSE

I asked myself and I refuse. Fanny, if you want to leave me and go away with this lean young fellow, I won't stand in your way.

MARIUS

And what happens to the child?

PANISSE

The child! The child! Why don't you ask me for my eyes,
my heart, my liver, my spleen? (FANNY *turns away*) No,
Marius! You will never get the little one. Never. (*Looks to*
FANNY *and goes to* MARIUS) Marius, you are young, you are
able to have other children. But this child, it's my first child—
my last child. You see Marius, if he were just an ordinary
child, like the children you see in the park. But this child is
so unique, so special! Cesar, tell him!

CESAR

He's right about that, Marius. You were a very beautiful
child, but this one . . .

PANISSE

He coughed!

FANNY

He coughed?

CESAR

I didn't hear anything.

PANISSE

No . . . no one hears him. But I hear him.
(*He runs into the nursery.* FANNY *follows and closes
door.*)

MARIUS

Panisse is a very generous and clever man, who says, "I
might give up the woman but I keep the child," knowing that

without the child the woman won't go. But is that fair? It's my child. I'm his father.

CESAR

Before he was born you were his father, but since his birth Panisse is his father.

MARIUS

Who is the father, the one who gives life or the one who buys the bibs?

CESAR

The father is the one who loves. Dogs give life too, and bulls give life. Besides, you were not looking to give life. You were looking for pleasure, and while you had pleasure the baby took life from you.
(*He sings*)
When the baby arrived, he weighed eight pounds.
Now he weighs twenty-three.
What are they made of, those extra pounds?
What can they be?
Fifteen pounds of love they are.
Fifteen solid pounds!
Fifteen pounds of caring and sharing and love.
Love is a very light thing.
Love is so fragile and frail.
You cannot hold it here in your hand
Or weigh it on a scale.
Cigarette smoke, that's all it is,
Wispy and curling around.
Oh, it takes a lot of love to make a pound.
(*Looks to* FANNY)

Fanny gave her measure. I slipped in an ounce or two. But the big weight . . . the bulk . . . Panisse.

> And yet, love is a very light thing.
> Light as a song in the air.
> How do you start
> To fill up a heart?
> How many ounces there?
> Dragon-fly wings—that's all it is,
> Whispering by with no sound.
> Oh, it takes a lot of love to make a pound.

How many of those fifteen pounds came from you, my son? How many?

MARIUS

I didn't even know a child had been born. I didn't have a chance to prove I loved him. But I have that chance now. I can go away. Good-bye, Father. Good-bye, Fanny.

(*Starts to go.* CESAR *takes both his shoulders, then holds his right arm.*)

FANNY

Marius, I want you to know something, and since your father is here to protect us against each other I'm going to tell you. When I saw you in that window I felt as if I were falling toward you, as you used to feel you were falling toward the sea.

CESAR

Fanny . . .

107

FANNY

(*Sings*)

When I look into my baby's eyes, I see your eyes.
When I see his smile, it is your own.
I would like to take your hand right now and follow
  you.
To happiness I've never known.
But, my dear, my dear, you know this dream can
  never be,
For other hands,
And other hearts
Are holding me,
Only you, long as I may live.

Think of this—each night there's a woman who would love
to lie down next to you and smell your hair and fall asleep
in the warmth of your body.

CESAR

Come on, my son, or you'll miss your train.

MARIUS

I wish I were in Panisse's shoes. When he misses his train,
he can come home.

CESAR

Don't blame Fanny for this. Pity her.
  (*Sings*)
      Here's a girl with no heart to give.

MARIUS

Worth every tear I'll cry!

CESAR

Fanny! Oh, Fanny!

FANNY, MARIUS, CESAR

Good-bye!
(MARIUS *starts to kiss her.* CESAR *pulls him away and shoves him out the door, then comes back and pats* FANNY's *cheek. She collapses.*)

Curtain

Scene III

Vignette 1

CESAR *and* PANISSE *come on pushing a large pram which obviously holds* CESARIO. *Other couples are pushing prams in the opposite direction.*

CESAR

He didn't catch the whooping cough last year because he was smart enough to sidestep it. (*A couple admire* CESARIO) He stops traffic.

YOUNG MAN

Promising young fellow you have there. Looks like his father.
   (CESAR *and* PANISSE *perk up and avoid each other's eyes.*)

CESAR

It might interest you to know that you are looking at the most important baby in France. He has three names.

PANISSE

Ending in Panisse.

YOUNG MAN

What do you think of our baby?

110

FANNY

CESAR
(*Noticing they have a baby*)
Very nice.
(*The couple exit, disappointed.*)

PANISSE
(*As he and* CESAR *exit*)
The parks are littered with babies like that.

Vignette 2

A group of townspeople are singing "Oysters, Cockles and Mussels." The light comes up on a fish stall. A well-dressed customer appears. It is HONORINE.

HONORINE
(*Pretending*)
I don't like the look of these oysters!
(*She laughs.*)

ALL

Hello, Honorine!
(*She greets everyone, shakes hands with some.*)

FISHWIFE

Oh, hello, Madame Cabinis. We've been saving something special for Panisse's big new house on the hill. Is the mayor coming to dinner?

HONORINE

We haven't asked him! (*She laughs*) Go get yourself a glass of wine. I'll take over. (*The woman goes*) I'm dying to get

111

my hands on those oysters. I want to see if I've lost my touch. (*She has put on the woman's apron. As she moves off with the crowd*) I could hardly wait to get down to this filthy, smelly waterfront!

> (*As they move off, the next vignette starts on the other side of the stage.*)

Vignette 3

CESAR *and* PANISSE *come on on bicycles.* PANISSE *is lagging behind.*

CESAR

What's the matter now?

PANISSE

I have a tendency to puff. Does he expect us to bicycle up that hill?

CESAR

He did.

PANISSE

Listen, you follow him over the hill and I'll go around and meet you on the other side.

CESAR

What would you do without me?

PANISSE

Don't tell Cesario I cheated about the hill. I want to get credit for climbing it too.

112

CESAR

You got credit for lots of things. You might as well get credit for this little hill too.

(CESAR *bicycles off.* PANISSE *follows on his bicycle, wobbling a little.*)

SCENE IV

Cesario's Room.

It is the room of a twelve-year-old boy. There are gay posters on the wall and all sorts of toys scattered around the room.

CESARIO is looking out the window when HONORINE enters. She is now gray-haired and very dignified.

HONORINE
(Sitting on the bed)

Cesario!
> *(She motions him to her.)*

CESARIO

They're putting up the ropes! *(He sits on the bed beside her)* I asked Father to take me to a circus. I didn't ask him to bring a circus to me.

HONORINE

It's a nice little traveling circus. Panisse and Son have always made their tents for them, so they're coming to honor your birthday.

CESARIO

Is Father still angry about the waterfront?

FANNY

HONORINE

He certainly is! And we must stick to our story. I'll make it up to you. After the party I'll come back up and read to you. We'll brush up on last month's deposits. (*Enter* PANISSE, CESAR *and* FANNY, *followed by* BRUN *and* ESCARTIFIQUE) Hello, everyone! Arithmetic lesson!

FANNY

(To all of them)

Please don't let's continue with this thing. The doctor told Panisse to take a rest before the party.

PANISSE

I cannot rest, eat, drink or enjoy parties until I know exactly what happened this morning.

FANNY

Oh, dear! Guests are arriving. Mama, tell us everything quickly and put Panisse's mind at ease.

HONORINE

Cesario and I spent the whole morning . . .

PANISSE

Looking at oysters! Yes, I've heard that story, but I don't believe anyone could look at oysters for five hours.

CESAR

(To CESARIO)

Don't be afraid. Tell us the truth.

115

FANNY

PANISSE

Honorine, did you let him out of your sight?

HONORINE

Yes, I did. I wanted him to run and play and have some
fun—and I wanted to have some fun myself. I'm still young
and full of vitality, and I don't care who knows it!

PANISSE

We all know it, Mother dear, but pull it in for just a
minute. (*To* CESARIO) So you went to the waterfront alone,
my boy—the one thing we begged you never to do.

CESARIO

I'm sorry, Father, but I didn't do anything bad.

CESAR

Did you meet anyone?

CESARIO

Yes—a very interesting admiral.
          (*Everyone exchanges looks.*)

PANISSE

What did you talk about?

CESARIO

I asked him about the sea.

PANISSE

The sea? Why?

CESARIO

Because a relation of mine went to sea.

PANISSE

Relation?

CESARIO

Yes. Marius . . . Cesar's son. Well, he's not really a relation, but Cesar's my godfather, so . . .

FANNY

(*Takes* CESARIO's *shoulder*)
Let's go downstairs. Please!

CESAR

(*Crossing to* CESARIO)
What do you know about my son?

CESARIO

Not much, except every time his name comes up, everybody sneezes or coughs or something. Did Marius do something bad?

CESAR

My son ran away from me.

CESARIO

Are you still angry with him?

117

CESAR

Yes, I believe so. I think that's how I'm able to live without him.

CESARIO

Did you know him, Father?

PANISSE

Yes, I knew him.

CESARIO

Didn't you like him?

PANISSE

Yes. Yes, I rather did like him.

CESARIO

Did you know him, Mama?

FANNY

(*Her arm around him*)
Of course. I used to sell fish next door to Cesar's bar. Marius and I grew up together.

CESARIO

Did you like him?

FANNY

Very much.

118

CESARIO

Well, if you all like him so much, why can't we invite him to my birthday party?

CESAR

We don't know where he is. He hasn't written us for years.

CESARIO

If I went to sea—(PANISSE *rises*)—would everybody be angry at me? Because that's all I want to do.

HONORINE

Now don't blame me for this. He doesn't tell me his secrets!
(*A general argument develops.*)

FANNY

Mama! Please, go downstairs, take care of the guests! (*She herds all but* CESARIO *out of the room. She turns back to* CESARIO, *who has his head in his hands, crying. She holds him*) Darling, what's the matter?

CESARIO

I'm sorry. I didn't mean to make so much trouble.

FANNY

You didn't make any trouble. Darling, you've got to understand something about all of us. We're grownups, and grownups are very strange people—unpredictable, confused, never knowing what they want.

CESARIO

I've noticed that about them.

FANNY

Have you? Then you can sympathize with us.
  (*She sings*)
      Here's a piece of good advice
      Think it over once or twice.
      Be kind to your parents
      Though they don't deserve it.
      Remember they're grownups,
      A difficult stage of life.
      They're apt to be nervous,
      And over-excited,
      Confused from their daily storm and strife.
      Just keep in mind,
      Though it sounds odd, I know,
      Most parents once were children long ago.
      Incredible!
      So treat them with patience
      And sweet understanding
      In spite of the foolish things they do.
      Some day you may wake up

120

FANNY

And find you're a parent too.
(CESARIO *gets a chair and seats* FANNY *in it. He stands
beside her and they sing another chorus of the song.
When the song ends:*)

FANNY

Oh, my goodness, the circus is beginning. You brush your
hair and come downstairs.
(*She exits.* CESARIO *starts to brush his hair. After a moment, the* ADMIRAL'S *duffelbag comes flying through
the window.* CESARIO *turns as the* ADMIRAL *enters.*)

CESARIO

Admiral!

ADMIRAL

(*Sings*)
I'm in love with an octopus . . .

I dug up a birthday present for you.
(*He digs around in his bag and brings out the same
sea shell* MARIUS *once showed to* FANNY.)

CESARIO

What a beauty!

ADMIRAL

Marius gave it to me when he went to sea.

CESARIO

Where is Marius now?

ADMIRAL

Don't tell anyone—(*He runs up to the door to make sure no one is listening*)—but he's working in a garage down the coast. I see him every week—bring him news from Marseille. I'm his newspaper.

CESARIO

Would you take me to see him some time?

ADMIRAL

He's going to America tomorrow.

CESARIO

Then there's only tonight—and they're giving this party for me.

ADMIRAL

With so many people around, you could easily sneak away. We could be back before the party's over.

CESARIO

The grownups will be dancing late. I'll take a chance. You hide in the garden and I'll wait until they're having a very good time—and then—*zip!*

ADMIRAL

Zip!

(*The curtains close.*)

Scene V

The Circus.

A group of clowns enter, followed by HONORINE, PANISSE, CESAR, FANNY, CESARIO *and other children, all on their way to the circus. They cross the stage as the music plays.*

The curtains open and we are inside a gaily-striped circus tent.

As the guests take their seats at one side, a colorful parade of clowns, masked figures, pretty girls and acrobats enters and marches about the stage.

Two trained seals are brought in and do their tricks to the great delight of the children.

An acrobat is lowered from the top of the tent and twirls on a rope as the entire circus personnel join in a dance below him. This reaches a climax and comes to a stop. Everyone applauds.

PANISSE

Cesario, come here and meet the people from the circus! (CESARIO *has slipped away with the* ADMIRAL *during the rope twirling act.* PANISSE *looks about wildly for him, then points off stage*) Cesario! Cesario! Cesario!

> (*He collapses in the arms of* FANNY *and* CESAR. *Everyone is calling for* CESARIO. *Servants and guests run off in great confusion. The music reaches a crescendo as the curtains close.*)

123

Scene VI

A Garage in Toulon.
MARIUS *is working at a bench. He wears overalls and looks older and more serious.* LOUIS *enters.*

LOUIS

Why work so hard on your last night?

MARIUS

I want to finish up.

LOUIS

Why don't you go out with one of your girls? Never knew a fellow with so many girls.

MARIUS

Well, you know how it is, Louis. When you can't get one you have to settle for a lot.

LOUIS

Yes, but who was *the* one?

MARIUS

Never mind.

LOUIS

Well, good-bye, Restless. (*They shake hands*) It's been nice knowing you.

124

(*As he goes out, the* ADMIRAL *enters from the other side with* CESARIO.)

MARIUS

Good night, Louis.

ADMIRAL

Hello, Marius.

MARIUS

Hello, Admiral.

ADMIRAL

Marius, this is Cesario Panisse. (MARIUS *rises and crosses toward* CESARIO) He wanted to see you before you go.
(*The* ADMIRAL *leaves.*)

MARIUS

You are Cesario.

CESARIO

And you're Marius.

MARIUS

Fanny's son . . .

CESARIO

Why do you look at me so funny? Aren't you going to shake hands or something?

MARIUS

Yes. (*They shake hands.* MARIUS *hugs the boy to him for a moment*) Excuse me, kid. Haven't seen anyone from home in so long . . .

125

CESARIO

Aren't you ever coming back to Marseille?

MARIUS

No. I'm going to America.
(*He sits on the bench.*)

CESARIO

(*Sits on a pile of tires by the bench and thinks for a moment*)
Would you take me with you?

MARIUS

To America?

CESARIO

Yes. I want to go to sea. Couldn't you take me? Teach me all about the sea? All the things you've learned?

MARIUS

The only thing I've ever learned is what I'm learning right now—that the worst thing that could happen to you would be to go with me.

CESARIO

But you love the sea, and I do too!

MARIUS

I ran away on an impulse just the way you want to do now, and I've regretted it ever since.

CESARIO

Why?

MARIUS

Because . . . Look—you've got a beautiful mother, the most wonderful woman in the world. And you're lucky to have a father like Panisse. Just looking at you and hearing you talk makes me know how much he's done for you. Suppose you had a father like me—chief cook and bottle-washer at sea, and jack-of-all-trades on land. I was a prize fighter for a while, a deep-sea diver—I was in the army. Nothing lasted. Once I left home, I never had another. How would you like a life like that?

CESARIO

It sounds wonderful! Take me with you!

MARIUS

Not a chance.

CESARIO

(*With spirit*)

Maybe I'll go anyway. I'll stow away!

MARIUS

What's that?

CESARIO

Don't you like me enough to take me with you?

MARIUS

(*Turning away*)

No!

CESARIO

Oh, please! Please! (MARIUS *turns back, looks at him, much tempted*) Please take me with you! Will you? Will you?

(MARIUS *puts his hand on the boy's head. The lights fade on them as the next scene starts.*)

Scene VII

Panisse's Bedroom.

PANISSE *is asleep in the bed. In the room are* BRUN, ESCARTI-FIQUE, HONORINE. CESAR *enters.*

HONORINE

Did they find Cesario?

CESAR

No, but everybody's looking for him—Fanny, the servants
. . . Has the doctor been here? (HONORINE *nods*) What did he
say?

ESCARTIFIQUE

Cooked.

CESAR

Poor old Panisse.

ESCARTIFIQUE

Of course, the doctor told him he was cooked ten years
ago and he got so mad he got right out of bed.

BRUN

What would make him mad enough to get out of bed this
time?

FANNY

CESAR

I know! We'll ask him to make a last confession. That will make him furious.

(*They all whisper.*)

PANISSE

It adds considerably to the strain of dying to try and hear what you're saying. Stop whispering. Speak up.

CESAR

Who's dying?

PANISSE

It's not dying I mind. It's giving up life that annoys me. You know what I'll miss most?

CESAR

What?

PANISSE

I'll miss the little pleasures in life—lunch, dinner . . . shaving in front of my window in the morning—looking out over the old port.

(*He dozes off.*)

CESAR

Panisse!

PANISSE

(*Waking*)

What!

130

CESAR

Keep talking! When you keep quiet like that we don't know what to expect.

PANISSE

Well, don't expect me to die yet, because I haven't decided when.

CESAR

It's not up to you.

PANISSE

Did you ever hear of the will to live?

CESAR

Yes, but I don't believe in it.

PANISSE
(*Strong*)

Well, you're not the one who's dying. I'll go when it's time to go—not a moment sooner.

CESAR

All right, all right! (*Aside to the others*) He's mad as hell! (*To* PANISSE) In the meantime, just to be on the safe side, how about a word or two with the priest?

PANISSE

No last confession.

CESAR

But you've got to make a last confession—otherwise the fat would be in the fire for good.

PANISSE

That remark was in extremely poor taste.

CESAR

I'm sorry.

PANISSE

But it was funny! What would the priest ask me?

CESAR

Oh, nothing. The Ten Commandments—that sort of thing.

PANISSE

The Ten Commandments? I'm all right on those. How do they go?

CESAR

Let's see . . . Thou shalt not kill.

PANISSE

Oh, I'm in wonderful shape on that one. When I think of all the times I wanted to kill you and didn't. I ought to get extra credit on that one.

CESAR

We'll both get promoted on that one.

132

PANISSE

This might be easier than I thought. Try another one.

BRUN

Thou shalt not steal.

CESAR

Ha ha!

PANISSE

Now these priests have got to understand that when you're in business and you're trying to raise a growing boy . . .

CESAR

All right—all right!

ESCARTIFIQUE

Say, aren't we getting close to that one about . . .

HONORINE

Yes, how are you on *that* one, Panisse?

PANISSE

Honorine, would you please leave the room for a minute?

HONORINE

I have to leave now, just when we're getting somewhere!
(*She goes. They all sit next to* PANISSE's *bed, eager to hear.*)

ESCARTIFIQUE

Now let's get to the point! Thou shalt not commit adultery —and speak up in a loud clear voice.

PANISSE

Now don't make light of this. Fanny has always been very fond of me, but as for passion, she never felt that for me.

CESAR

We do understand.

PANISSE

So of course I respected her feeling and I've been very— undemanding, so to speak.

ESCARTIFIQUE

And so?

PANISSE

And so, naturally . . .

ESCARTIFIQUE

Naturally!

PANISSE

The devil found in me a good customer, if you know what I mean.

CESAR

He tempted you, hm?

134

PANISSE

You might put it that way.

ESCARTIFIQUE

And what form did this temptation take?

PANISSE

It took the form of one of my lady employees.

CESAR

Which one?

PANISSE

The little redhead!

CESAR

I'll be damned and blasted.

PANISSE

What are you so amazed at?

CESAR

Not at you—at that redhead. When I asked her, she slapped my face!

PANISSE

Revenge! Revenge! This gives me a new lease on life!
(*He climbs out of bed.* BRUN, ESCARTIFIQUE *and* CESAR *rush to his side.* FANNY *runs in.*)

FANNY

Panisse, what are you doing out of bed?

PANISSE

Did you find the boy?

FANNY

(*Rushes to his side*)

No, but you're a very sick man. Please get back in bed, Panisse.

MARIUS

(*Off stage*)

Hello! Is there anybody home in this house? Where the devil is everybody? (*Everybody freezes*) Hello, there!

CESAR

It may be the priest.

PANISSE

The priest? You know that voice as well as I.

MARIUS

(*Off stage, but nearer*)

Hello, there! (*A knock at the door. No one moves. The door opens and* MARIUS *enters, holding* CESARIO *by the collar*) Did anyone lose a boy? He didn't want to come home, but here he is.

136

PANISSE

Oh, they look well together.
(*He collapses in* CESAR's *arms and the curtain falls.*)

*   *   *   *   *

Before the curtain, a PRIEST *crosses with an* ALTAR BOY. *The* ADMIRAL *is crossing in the opposite direction.*

ADMIRAL

Oh, Father. Tell Panisse that Marius sailed for America. He doesn't have to worry about us any more.
(*They exit in opposite directions.*)

*   *   *   *   *

PANISSE *is in the bed. He and* CESAR *are playing cards.*

PANISSE

Another king? How do you always manage to pull the card you need when you need it?

CESAR

Don't you wish you knew?

PANISSE

Please tell me, Cesar.

CESAR

Promise not to tell anyone?

FANNY

PANISSE

Who am I going to tell—the angel Gabriel?

CESAR

Look. I don't pull it off the top—I pull it off the bottom.
(*Drops card.*)

PANISSE

Oh! Let me try it.
(*He does.*)

CESAR

Perfect!

PANISSE

(*Gives card back to* CESAR)
Oh, that's a very satisfactory feeling. I hope Gabriel plays cards.

CESAR

(*Puts cards on board at* PANISSE's *feet*)
You'll be able to cheat the cloud right from under him.

PANISSE

Is Fanny with the boy?

CESAR

Yes.

PANISSE

Did you have a chance to visit with Marius before he left?

138

CESAR

Yes. I even asked him why he never got married. He said he didn't know.

PANISSE

I know. (*Pause*) Cesar, I've done a lot of confessing lately, but there's one thing I'd like to confess to you.

CESAR

(*Picks up board*)

Let's play another game.

PANISSE

In a minute. Cesar, you always cheated me at cards when we played for a few francs, but when we were playing for big stakes, I cheated you.

(*Touches* CESAR'S *arm*.)

CESAR

You're not confessing—you're bragging.

PANISSE

Do you remember the day you wanted to send for Marius and you and Fanny were so distraught—that day I outplayed you. I kept you from sending for Marius.

CESAR

(*Pats his knee*)

Don't feel guilty about that. I was so angry with him for running away that I let you outplay me.

PANISSE

Now you're bragging. I want to write Marius a letter. Will you take it down? (CESAR *picks up the pen and places pad on cardboard.* PANISSE *dictates*) "Dear Marius. This is a proposal of marriage. Will you do me the honor to marry my wife? She will be free soon—"

CESAR

(*To* PANISSE)

Oh, come on!

PANISSE

"—and I recommend her very highly. I will rest easier knowing she has someone to care for her, especially if it's the one she has always loved." How does that sound?

CESAR

(*Looking up*)

It's so good he'll think I wrote it.

PANISSE

"I also feel that my son should have a father, even though it's his own."

CESAR

You know I'm beginning to like this letter. Go on.

PANISSE

"I hope you will agree and not be stubborn like that old rhinoceros, your father." (CESAR *stops writing*) Why aren't you putting that down?

140

CESAR

I cannot spell rhinoceros.

PANISSE

All right, leave it out, but it kills the style of the whole letter.

CESAR

I cannot help it. Go on.

PANISSE

"Hastily yours." (*He signs the letter*) Will you promise to send it the moment the time comes?

CESAR

(*Tears off page and gets envelope. Puts cardboard on bench*)
I'll send it off. But you can't go, Panisse. I won't be any good without you. Who am I going to fight with?

PANISSE

There's Brun. There's Escartifique.

CESAR

They are not Panisses.
   (*Puts letter in envelope.*)

PANISSE

One more thing—about the boy. Cesar, would you mind if your grandson keeps the name Panisse?

141

CESAR

Of course not. (*Holds the letter*) Thanks to you, there will be others.

PANISSE

Others! And now, tell me about the furniture.

CESAR

The furniture?

PANISSE

(*He sings*)
Welcome home, says the street,
As I hurry on my way.

CESAR

Welcome home, sings the gate, like a song.
Welcome home, says the door,
Glad to feel your hand once more,
Now you're back where you belong.
Welcome home, says the chair,
Holding out its friendly arms.
Welcome home, says the bed,
Rest on me.
(CESAR *turns and looks at* PANISSE, *realizes he has died,
and places* PANISSE's *hand on his chest*)
Now you're back where you should be,

FANNY

Close your eyes, close your eyes,
And the world will settle down to size . . .
(*The music continues.* CESAR *is looking at the letter as the curtain comes down.*)